Listening Skills

BY
DAVID W. WILSON, PH.D., AND RUTH ANN WILSON

COPYRIGHT © 1998 Mark Twain Media, Inc.

Printing No. CD–1898

Mark Twain Media, Inc., Publishers
Distributed by Carson-Dellosa Publishing Company, Inc.

The purchase of this book entitles the buyer to reproduce the student pages for classroom use only. Other permissions may be obtained by writing Mark Twain Media, Inc., Publishers.

All rights reserved. Printed in the United States of America.

Table of Contents

Introduction 1

Improving Your Listening Behavior: Tips for Students 2

Thinking About Listening 5
    What Does a Good Listener Do? 5
    The Importance and Benefits of Listening 6
    What Could Happen? 8
    The Right and Wrong of It 10
    What Should You Do? 12
    Poor Excuses for Not Listening 13
    "Now Hear This!" 14
    What Does This Mean? 15
    People Who Are Good Listeners 16
    Hurricane Warning! 17

Self-Analysis 18
    How Much Time Do You Spend Listening? 18
    Are You a Good Listener? 19
    Checking Your Attitude Toward Listening 21
    Identifying Your Listening Strengths and Weaknesses 23
    Setting Goals and Making Plans 26

Practicing Listening 27
    Listening Carefully 27
    Listening for the Truth 29
    Comparing Notes of Two People Listening to the Same Thing 30
    Interviewing a Classmate 31
    Listening to Commercials 33
    Following Directions 35
    Listening for Sounds All Around 36
    Group Discussion 37
    Interviewing a "Listener" From Your Community 38
    Listening to the Evening News 39
    Who Am I? 40
    It's in the Bag! 42
    Listen to the Middle Man 43
    Poster-Making 44
    When Nobody Listens 45
    Listening or Not Listening? 47
    Name That Word 48
    Mixed-Up Charades 49
    Trading Places Game 50
    Who Said That Silly Sentence? 51
    Can You Answer Questions After Listening? 52
    Famous Mystery Person 54

Tips for the Teacher 56

Bibliography 61

Introduction

Education is, to a large degree, a matter of communication. Students learn through writing, reading, speaking, and listening. It is the latter form of communication that forms the substance of this book. Listening is, in fact, the most used form of communication, especially in the classroom (Barker, 1971). But good listening is more than just a student behavior that facilitates learning. Indeed, it is a behavior that warrants the status of an educational objective.

Unfortunately, for many students, good listening does not "just happen." Students need training and practice in listening. What teacher has not exclaimed, "If my students would only listen!"? While poor listening can have a physical or even emotional basis, it is more often a matter of too little motivation (i.e., choosing not to listen or not making listening a high priority), a distracting environment, or simply not knowing how to listen well. The good listener is motivated to listen, knows how to optimize the listening environment, and makes listening a habit.

With these things in mind, this book attempts to motivate students, inform them, and involve them in interesting activities by which they can practice good listening. The book is a resource for teachers who know all too well the difference between hearing and listening. Teachers, of course, spend a great deal of classroom time playing the role of speaker. Unless there are attentive, willing, and capable listeners on the receiving end, communication breaks down, and so does, by definition, education.

The book is organized as follows: The first section offers students tips for improving their listening behavior. The second section contains a number of activities that involve students in thinking about listening. The third section includes activities that ask students to analyze their own listening habits. The fourth section consists of activities that give students practice in listening. Finally, the fifth section is a set of tips for teachers on how to facilitate good listening.

—The Authors—

Improving Your Listening Behavior: Tips for Students

Listening is an important and necessary skill for your success as a student. You can improve your listening effectiveness through <u>practice</u>. But first, you must <u>learn</u> what it takes to be a good listener and be <u>motivated</u> to listen. Good listening is a matter of self-discipline. Whether you listen is up to you. No one can do it for you. Make good listening a goal and then begin working on a plan to correct your listening problems. Focus on trying to improve your listening behavior. Even if you are already a good listener, you can find ways to improve. Here are some suggestions:

Make Listening a Goal:

- **Make listening an important personal goal.** Make it something you <u>want</u> to do. Make it a habit. <u>Decide</u> to improve your listening.

- **Be willing to work at listening.** Listening is hard work and takes effort.

- **Pay attention at all times.** Keep your concentration on the speaker's <u>message</u>.

- **Listen in a complete way.** Give the speaker your undivided attention. For example, don't be planning what you are going to say next. If you do, you may miss part of what the speaker says.

- **Listen with an open mind.** If you have your mind made up about something or have decided you already know all you need to know, you may miss out on some very valuable, new information. Do not let any biases you have keep you from listening to what the speaker has to say.

- **Get interested in the speaker's topic.** Good listeners find ways of getting interested and staying interested in the speaker's topic. Know why the information is important or useful. Listen for unusual or exciting things. Listen for memorable quotations. Focus on visual aids like pictures and charts.

Listen Courteously:

- **Be a courteous listener.** A courteous listener pays attention, is not rude to the speaker, and listens even if he or she disagrees with the speaker. A courteous listener does not pretend to listen; he or she truly listens.

- **Show the speaker you are ready to listen.** Sit up straight, face the speaker, look at him or her, do not cross your arms or hide behind a pile of books, and look enthusiastic and interested.

- **Listen quietly.** Do not fidget, shuffle your feet, play with things, or make noises.

- **Do not interrupt the speaker.** Be patient. Offer your comments or ask your questions only when the speaker has finished speaking and it is your turn to speak.

- **Do not distract others.** Everyone else needs to listen just as you do.

- **Give the speaker feedback.** Nod your head occasionally. When appropriate, ask questions related to what the speaker said, express an opinion, or make other relevant comments. Or, if appropriate, interject brief comments like, "Yes" or "I see."

- **In a group discussion, listen willingly and courteously to other points of view.** Recognize the right of other people to hold opinions that differ from yours. Be willing to acknowledge that others may know things that you do not.

- **In a group discussion, offer feedback to show others you have been listening.** When it is your turn to speak, briefly summarize what was just said. Begin by saying something like, "If I understood you correctly, you said…" or "Correct me if I'm wrong, but you seem to be saying…." After such a statement, contribute to the discussion with your own comments. When you give such feedback, previous speakers have an opportunity to discover whether you correctly understood what they said. And it gives others an opportunity to clarify their comments if needed and to correct any misperceptions.

Think About the Speaker's Message:

- **Think about what you are hearing and try to understand it.** Ask yourself questions like: What is the main idea being presented? What is the speaker's purpose (to persuade me? to inform me?)? Is the information being presented accurate and up-to-date? Does it make sense? Why is this important? How does the speaker know this? Is the idea being presented good or bad? Is the speaker presenting facts, opinions, or both? Is the speaker biased in any way? What conclusions can I draw from the speaker's presentation?

- **Realize that you can think faster than the speaker can talk.** Use this extra "thinking time" to think about the speaker's message. For example, ask yourself questions about what you just heard: "Does this fit with what I already know or read in the text?" "What would be a good example of that?" Do not use the "free time" to worry about something, finish a book report, or plan your after-school activities.

- **Listen with a purpose in mind.** Listen <u>for</u> something. For example, listen to learn or listen to evaluate.

- **Mentally organize the information you are hearing.** When you see how things are connected and how one thing follows directly and logically from another, it is easier to listen.

- **Ask for clarification when you do not understand what was said.**

- **Listen to remember.** You can do this by not only paying close attention, but also by attaching meaning to what you are hearing and mentally organizing it. Seek accuracy in what you remember. Taking notes may help you do this.

- **Give meaning to what you are hearing by interpreting it.** Listen for the main ideas. Listen for supporting details and examples. Listen carefully so you can tell the difference between what is important and what is irrelevant. Listen for answers to questions you had in mind. Think about how the information is useful. Relate the material to other things you are aware of. As you listen, try to mentally summarize what you have heard up to that point.

- **Be personally involved in the speaker's message.** As you are listening, relate the information to your own experiences and think of ways that the message has meaning for you. How could you apply the information to your own life and use it in some way?

- **Do not focus on the speaker's appearance and personal characteristics or whether you like the speaker.** If you concentrate on the speaker's tone of voice, clothing, hair color, or personality, you will not remember the message.

Use Strategies to Make Listening Easier:

- **Be well-rested and healthy.** It is hard to listen when you are tired or sick.

- **Eliminate obstacles to good listening.** If your classroom is too hot, ask the teacher to turn on a fan or open a window. Work to eliminate any background noise. If you cannot actually get rid of an outside distraction, try to mentally block it out. With some listening difficulties, adjustments on your part can help. For example, if your teacher has a soft voice and is difficult to hear, ask him or her if you can sit in a location where it is easier to hear.

- **Avoid self-distractions.** Do not talk, sing, draw, doodle, read, or look out the window. Concentrate on one thing—the speaker's message.

- **Build your vocabulary.** Good listening requires that you understand what you are hearing. Otherwise, you may find yourself "tuning out" and ignoring the speaker.

- **Become familiar with the topic.** In the classroom setting, you can do this by reading relevant assignments before your teacher talks about the same material in class.

- **If you are taking notes, have paper and pencil ready to go.** But do not let note-taking distract you from careful listening. Do not take down every word the speaker says; instead, write down the most important points.

Listening Skills — What Does a Good Listener Do?

Name: Louis Forlit   Date: _____

What Does a Good Listener Do?

A good listener **wants to listen**, **enjoys listening**, **thinks it is important to listen**, and **tries to listen**. The good listener **blocks out distractions** and **concentrates on listening to the speaker's message**. The good listener **makes listening a personal goal**, **practices good listening every day**, and **makes listening a habit**.

1. In your own words, describe a good listener. (In other words, in a listening situation, what is a good listener doing?)

   Someone who listens to the speaker and tries and does block out disturbsions.

2. Describe a poor listener.

   Someone who talks and daydreams often.

3. Can you "hear" someone but still not really "listen"? Explain.

   Yes, but most of the time my mine will be on something else.

Reflection:

What did you learn from this activity?

How to be a good listener.

How will what you learned make you a better listener?

Pay attention, follow directions.

Listening Skills   The Importance and Benefits of Listening

Name _____ Date _____

The Importance and Benefits of Listening

Every day of your life, listening is an important activity. When you listen, you do not just hear something—you attend to it carefully and think about it. You try to understand and interpret it. Just like reading, listening is an important way in which you learn about the world. For example, much of what you learn at school comes through listening.

For most students, listening carefully in the classroom is not always an easy thing to do. Good listening requires that you ignore all distractions and concentrate solely on what the teacher or other speaker is saying. Because this can be a difficult thing to do, listening is a skill that you must work at and practice every day. It is a skill you can improve.

Fortunately, your efforts at becoming a better listener can have important and immediate benefits. For one thing, good listening can help you learn new words and improve your speaking skills. But, more generally, being a good listener can help earn your teacher's respect, help your performance on exams, and help you earn better grades in school. Because good listening helps you learn, listening can help you not only in the classroom, but also in life in general.

Benefits of Listening in the Classroom:

1. How can good listening help you complete a math assignment correctly?
   Write the assignment down, and pay attention to the teacher.

2. Explain why good listening helps students make better grades.
   They can tune out distractions and listen carefully.

3. Can you think of other advantages of listening carefully in the classroom?
   Clear your mind and set it to what your teacher is trying to tell you.

4. What can happen to a student who does not listen well in the classroom?
   They can fail tests and work, and will not know what directions to do.

Other Benefits of Listening:

1. How can good listening help save you time?
   You don't have to sit there and think of what to do and waste time.

2. How can good listening keep you from making a mistake?
   You followed directions correctly and payed attention.

© Mark Twain Media, Inc., Publishers

Listening Skills   The Importance and Benefits of Listening

Name _Louis Foclet_____ Date _____

3. Do you think good listening can help you become a more mature person? Explain.
   Yes, You know what to do you don't have
   issues often of a hearing disorder.

4. How can good listening help you expand your interests and experiences?
   You learn more and ~~get~~ have better ideas
   about things.

5. How can good listening help you in a job someday?
   You know what to do in your job.
   _____

6. Listeners who are attentive and interested often cause a speaker to do a better job of presenting information than would be the case if the listeners seemed to be bored and disinterested. Why do you think that is?
   _____
   _____

7. List three types of situations in which you have learned something important by listening.
   a) _____
   b) _____
   c) _____

8. Why is it important to you to have others listen when you are talking to them?
   _____
   _____

9. What do you think is the most important benefit of good listening? Why?
   _____
   _____

Reflection:

What did you learn from this activity?
_____
_____
_____

How will what you learned make you a better listener?
_____
_____

© Mark Twain Media, Inc., Publishers

Listening Skills — What Could Happen?

Name _____ Date _____

What Could Happen?

For each situation described below, indicate some of the problems that could result if the situation did, in fact, occur.

1. What could happen if you did not listen carefully to your doctor's instructions?

_____
_____
_____

2. What could happen if you did not listen carefully to important homework assignment instructions given to you by your teacher?

_____
_____
_____

3. What could happen if you did not listen carefully to the directions someone gave you when you were lost in an unfamiliar city?

_____
_____
_____
_____

4. What could happen if you did not listen carefully when someone was introduced to you?

_____
_____
_____
_____

Listening Skills   What Could Happen?

Name _____ Date _____

5. What could happen if you did not listen carefully when your friend had a problem and wanted to talk to you about it?

_____

_____

_____

6. What could happen if you did not listen carefully when your parents explained to you what they wanted you to do and why?

_____

_____

_____

7. Think of a time when you did not listen carefully. What happened?

_____

_____

_____

Reflection:

What did you learn from this activity?

_____

_____

How will what you have learned make you a better listener?

_____

_____

_____

Listening Skills   The Right and Wrong of It

Name _____ Date _____

The Right and Wrong of It

In each situation below, describe what the student did right and what the student did wrong.

1. The teacher, Mr. Jones, is explaining how to do an assignment. Nicole, who is sitting at the back of the room, cannot hear, so she asks the student in front of her, "What is Mr. Jones saying?"

What, if anything, did Nicole do right?
_____
_____

What, if anything, did Nicole do wrong?
_____
_____

2. While the teacher is speaking to the class, Jake raises his hand and asks her if he can leave to go to the restroom. The teacher gives him permission to do so. On the way out of the room, Jake whispers something funny to some of his friends.

What, if anything, did Jake do right?
_____
_____

What, if anything, did Jake do wrong?
_____
_____

3. The teacher invites a guest speaker to class. The man has a speech problem that makes it difficult for him to properly pronounce some words. Students in the class giggle when the speaker makes such mistakes. After the talk, the students give the speaker a round of applause and ask questions.

What, if anything, did the students do right?
_____
_____

What, if anything, did the students do wrong?
_____
_____

4. The teacher is giving a social studies lecture on the Civil War. Mary decided that since she read the assignment on the Civil War and knew the material very well, it was all right if she studied for her math test instead of listening to the lecture.

© Mark Twain Media, Inc., Publishers

Listening Skills   The Right and Wrong of It

Name _____ Date _____

What, if anything, did Mary do right?
_____
_____

What, if anything, did Mary do wrong?
_____
_____

5. Describe a real listening situation from your experience.
_____
_____
_____
_____

What, if anything, was done right?
_____
_____

What, if anything, was done wrong?
_____
_____
_____

Reflection:

What did you learn from this activity?
_____
_____
_____

How will what you learned make you a better listener?
_____
_____
_____

Listening Skills   What Should You Do?

Name _____ Date _____

What Should You Do?

For each situation below, describe what you should do to solve the problem that is causing you not to listen.

1. The sound is too low on a video your class is watching.
_____

2. You have a head cold today and cannot hear the speaker.
_____

3. A guest speaker is talking too softly.
_____

4. Other students are bothering and distracting you from paying attention to the teacher.
_____

5. You are listening and taking notes when your pen runs out of ink. You lose your concentration.
_____

6. You notice the speaker's pants are ripped and think it is funny.
_____

7. You are listening to the speaker, but you cannot follow what he or she is saying because the presentation seems to be disorganized. You are confused.
_____

8. Describe a problem that has, or could, come up to cause you to have a problem when listening.
_____
_____

What did or could you do to solve the problem?
_____

Reflection:

What did you learn from this activity?
_____
_____

How will what you learned make you a better listener?
_____
_____

Listening Skills   Poor Excuses for Not Listening

Name _____ Date _____

Poor Excuses for Not Listening

Explain why each of the following is a poor excuse for not listening.

1. "This is too hard. I don't understand what you're saying.": _____
_____

2. "I'm bored. This isn't interesting.": _____
_____

3. "I don't need to listen. I already know what I'm supposed to do.": _____
_____

4. "I can't listen. Everybody's making too much noise.": _____
_____

5. "He's bothering me. I can't concentrate.": _____
_____

6. "It's too hot to listen.": _____
_____

7. "I don't want to listen. It's almost lunch time and I'm hungry.": _____
_____

8. "The teacher is talking too fast. I can't keep up.": _____
_____

9. "The teacher is using too many words I don't know.": _____
_____

10. Think of an excuse for not listening that you have heard. What was the excuse? Explain why this is a poor excuse.
_____
_____
_____

Reflection:

What did you learn from this activity? _____
_____

How will what you learned make you a better listener? _____
_____

© Mark Twain Media, Inc., Publishers

Listening Skills   "Now Hear This!"

Name _____ Date _____

"Now Hear This!"

1. Right before speakers begin talking, they often say something like, "Now hear this!", "Listen up, folks!", or "May I have your attention, please?". Why do you think speakers say such things?

_____
_____
_____

2. Get with a partner to do this brainstorming activity. Write down as many things as you can think of that a speaker might say to get an audience to listen.

_____
_____
_____
_____
_____
_____
_____

3. If <u>you</u> were to give a speech and wanted others to listen carefully, how would you begin your remarks?

_____
_____
_____

Reflection:

What did you learn from this activity?

_____
_____
_____

How will what you learned make you a better listener?

_____
_____
_____

Listening Skills | **What Does This Mean?**

Name _____ Date _____

What Does This Mean?

With a partner, discuss and then write down what you think each of the following sentences mean.

1. She was only half-listening to what was being said.
_____

2. He was listening with one ear.
_____

3. He didn't hear you. His mind was somewhere else.
_____

4. She heard only what she <u>wanted</u> to hear.
_____

5. Whenever I start talking about that, he always turns a deaf ear.
_____

6. Please lend me an ear.
_____

7. Don't tune me out.
_____

8. They have ears, but they hear not.
_____

9. I know you believe you understand what you think I said, but I'm not sure you realize that what you heard is not what I meant.
_____

10. I'm all ears.
_____

Reflection:

What did you learn from this activity? _____

_____

How will what you learned make you a better listener? _____

_____

Name _____ Date _____

People Who Are Good Listeners

In this activity, think about people who are good listeners or at least need to be good listeners.

1. A person I know who is a good listener is: _____

I thought of this person because: _____
_____

2. Write why it is important for the following people to be good listeners:

a) Waitress: _____

b) Doctor: _____

c) Parent: _____

d) Airline pilot: _____

e) Juror: _____

f) Newspaper reporter: _____

g) Detective: _____

h) Basketball player: _____

i) School counselor: _____

j) Student: _____

Reflection:

What did you learn from this activity?
_____
_____
_____

How will what you learned make you a better listener?
_____
_____
_____
_____

Name _____ Date _____

Hurricane Warning!

In this activity, suppose it is your job to write an announcement to be read on the radio that warns listeners they should evacuate the area and seek secure shelter because of an impending hurricane. Your goals in writing such an announcement are to capture the listeners' attention, keep that attention, and convey a message with instructions that will be heard accurately, will be understood, and will be obeyed. What would you say in such an ad, and what techniques would you use to accomplish these goals?

Explain your ad and what you would do.

_____

_____

_____

_____

_____

_____

_____

_____

_____

_____

_____

Reflection:

What did you learn from this activity?

_____

_____

How will what you learned make you a better listener?

_____

_____

_____

How Much Time Do You Spend Listening?

Verbal communication occurs in the following ways: **reading**, **speaking**, **writing**, and **listening**.

During a typical day, how much of your time do you spend in each of these forms of communication? To find out, keep a record during one of your normal days and note how much time you are engaged in each of the activities. Of the total time you spend communicating, calculate the percentage of time spent in each type of communication. Next, using the percentage figures from each student in your class, calculate the class average for each of the categories. How do you compare? In the graph below, show your percentages compared to the class averages.

Form of Communication	Number of Hours	Percentage of Total	Class Average
Speaking	_____	_____	_____
Reading	_____	_____	_____
Writing	_____	_____	_____
Listening	_____	_____	_____

Communication Graph

Reflection:

What did you learn from this activity?

_____

_____

How will what you learned make you a better listener?

_____

Name _____ Date _____

Are You a Good Listener?

One way to find out if you are a good listener is to respond to the statements below. Circle the number and word or phrase that make each statement true for you.

When someone (for example, my teacher) is speaking to me:

1. I daydream.

0	1	2	3
never	rarely	often	very often

2. I think about what I want to say next.

0	1	2	3
never	rarely	often	very often

3. I make plans (for example, I plan what I will do after school).

0	1	2	3
never	rarely	often	very often

4. I talk to others around me.

0	1	2	3
never	rarely	often	very often

5. I am easily distracted by noises or other things going on around me.

0	1	2	3
never	rarely	often	very often

6. I worry about my problems.

0	1	2	3
never	rarely	often	very often

7. I interrupt the speaker.

0	1	2	3
never	rarely	often	very often

8. I fidget, squirm, doodle, and act disinterested.

0	1	2	3
never	rarely	often	very often

9. I go to sleep.

0	1	2	3
never	rarely	often	very often

10. I do not listen carefully.

0	1	2	3
never	rarely	often	very often

11. I pretend to listen.

0	1	2	3
never	rarely	often	very often

12. I look around the room more than I look at the speaker.

0	1	2	3
never	rarely	often	very often

© Mark Twain Media, Inc., Publishers

Listening Skills   Are You a Good Listener?

Name _____ Date _____

13. I don't listen carefully if I don't like what the speaker is saying.
         0   1   2   3
       never   rarely   often   very often

14. I don't listen carefully if I don't understand what is being said.
         0   1   2   3
       never   rarely   often   very often

15. I don't listen carefully when the speaker is correcting me.
         0   1   2   3
       never   rarely   often   very often

16. I don't listen carefully if the speaker acts disinterested or is unprepared.
         0   1   2   3
       never   rarely   often   very often

17. I don't listen carefully if the speaker is nervous.
         0   1   2   3
       never   rarely   often   very often

18. I don't listen carefully if the speaker acts strange or is wearing "funny" clothing.
         0   1   2   3
       never   rarely   often   very often

19. I don't listen carefully when the speaker constantly says "uh," "um," "er," and "you know."
         0   1   2   3
       never   rarely   often   very often

Now look back at your responses to the statements. If you circled never or rarely most of the time, it indicates that you are doing a pretty good job of listening. Did you circle often or very often for any of the items? The more times you did so, the more problems you seem to be having with listening.

Reflection:

What did you learn from this activity?

_____

_____

_____

How will what you learned make you a better listener?

_____

_____

_____

Listening Skills   Checking Your Attitude Toward Listening

Name _____ Date _____

Checking Your Attitude Toward Listening

Being a good listener is very dependent on your desire or motivation to listen. The items below should help you determine if you have a good attitude toward listening.

Indicate whether you basically agree (A) or disagree (D) with each of the following statements: (circle A or D)

A   D   1. I'd rather talk than listen.

A   D   2. I believe that being a good listener will help me be successful in life.

A   D   3. Listening is a waste of time.

A   D   4. I enjoy listening to other people's ideas.

A   D   5. Listening is boring.

A   D   6. I believe I can learn things by listening to others.

A   D   7. What I read is more important than what I hear.

A   D   8. Good listening can help me do well on exams in school.

A   D   9. Most people don't have anything worthwhile to say.

A   D   10. When I'm at school, I try hard to listen and understand what the teacher is saying.

A   D   11. Listening is too hard.

A   D   12. People who are good listeners earn the respect of others.

A   D   13. A person is either born a good listener or not; he or she cannot improve.

A   D   14. It frustrates me when other students make noise that keeps me from being able to hear the teacher.

A   D   15. It is more important to be a good speaker than a good listener.

A   D   16. I would like to improve my listening skills.

A   D   17. I don't like to listen to people when I disagree with them or dislike what they are saying.

Listening Skills   Checking Your Attitude Toward Listening

Name _____ Date _____

A   D   18. I think it is just as important, if not more important, to listen as it is to talk.

A   D   19. I don't like it when people tell me I should listen carefully.

A   D   20. I listen carefully even when the speaker's topic is not one of my favorites.

Look back now over your responses. How many of the 10 odd-numbered items did you disagree with? Fill in the number here:____. The more of these items you disagreed with, the more positive your attitude toward listening and the easier it will be for you to improve and overcome some of your difficulties.

How many of the 10 even-numbered items did you agree with? Fill in the number here: ____. The more of these items you agreed with, the more positive your attitude toward listening and, again, the easier it will be for you to improve and overcome some of your difficulties.

Reflection:

What did you learn from this activity?

_____
_____
_____

How will what you learned make you a better listener?

_____
_____
_____

Name _____ Date _____

Identifying Your Listening Strengths and Weaknesses

First, it is important to recognize that you may already have a number of strengths when it comes to listening. But, no doubt, there is also room for improvement. Before you can improve your listening skills, you must be aware of any listening difficulties you are currently having. Only with such an awareness can you make a plan to overcome your problems. The questions below ask you to think not only about your strengths as a listener, but about some of your difficulties as well.

1. In one or two sentences, describe the type of listener you are today.

_____
_____
_____

2. Would you describe yourself as a good listener? Why or why not?

_____
_____
_____

3. List some of your strengths with regard to listening. What do you do well?

_____
_____
_____

4. To what extent do you agree with the following statement? Circle your answer and then explain it.

"I am satisfied with my current ability to concentrate and listen to a speaker."

| Strongly Agree | Moderately Agree | Slightly Agree | Slightly Disagree | Moderately Disagree | Strongly Disagree |

Explanation: _____
_____
_____

5. Identify the three biggest problems you have when trying to listen in the classroom (for example, daydreaming).

a) _____

b) _____

c) _____

Listening Skills   Identifying Your Listening Strengths and Weaknesses

Name _____ Date _____

6. Describe the times or situations in which you have the greatest listening difficulties (for example, when your teacher is discussing a difficult topic).
_____
_____
_____

Why do you think these situations have been a problem for you?
_____
_____
_____

7. When you are listening to your teacher, what are you most distracted by (for example, noises or objects on your desk)?
_____
_____
_____

8. Describe the times or situations in which listening has been easy for you.
_____
_____
_____

Why do you think listening has been easy for you in these situations?
_____
_____
_____

9. Describe three ways in which listening difficulties have caused you problems.

a) _____

b) _____

c) _____

10. Have you ever listened to someone speak and almost immediately afterwards not been able to remember what the person said? Explain why such a thing might happen.
_____
_____
_____

© Mark Twain Media, Inc., Publishers

Listening Skills • Identifying Your Listening Strengths and Weaknesses

Name _____ Date _____

11. Do you have enough self-discipline to improve your listening? Explain.
_____
_____
_____

12. What needs your attention first as you try to improve your listening?
_____
_____
_____

Reflection:

What did you learn from this activity?
_____
_____
_____

How will what you learned make you a better listener?
_____
_____
_____

© Mark Twain Media, Inc., Publishers

Listening Skills   **Setting Goals and Making Plans**

Name _____ Date _____

Setting Goals and Making Plans

In this activity, think about what you can do to be a better listener in the future.

1. Describe in one or two sentences the type of listener you hope to be in the future.

_____

_____

_____

2. What steps can you take to overcome each difficulty you are currently having with respect to listening? For each listening problem you can identify for yourself, describe how you can overcome it.

Problem: _____

Solution: _____

Problem: _____

Solution: _____

Problem: _____

Solution: _____

Problem: _____

Solution: _____

3. Who could help you solve your listening problems? Explain.

_____

_____

4. Set a goal, which you will try to achieve this year, to overcome a listening problem.

My goal: _____

_____

Reflection:

What did you learn from this activity?

_____

_____

How will what you learned make you a better listener?

_____

_____

Listening Skills   Listening Carefully

Name _____ Date _____

Listening Carefully

Working in small groups, cut apart and pass out the question cards below. Each group member should read a question to the group. You may read only your own card, but you may read it to the group as many times as necessary. Other group members must listen carefully. Discuss the question in your group and then agree upon an answer. Record your answers on the answer sheet.

1. You want to build a 100-foot wire fence with 10 feet between the poles. How many fence poles will you need?

2. What was your teacher's name five years ago?

3. You are in a dark cabin with a candle, an oil lamp, and a fireplace. If you have only one match, what should you light first?

4. A rancher had a herd of 196 cows. All but 51 died. How many cows does he have left?

5. A plane crashed on the border between Kansas and Nebraska. In which state were the survivors buried?

6. Seven months have 31 days. How many months have 28 days?

7. How far can a man run into a jungle?

8. Do they have a fourth of July in Canada?

Answers found on page 60.

Name _____ Date _____

Answer Sheet for Listening Carefully Activity

Group members: _____
_____

Write the answers to your question cards below. Explain each answer.

1. _____
_____

2. _____
_____

3. _____
_____

4. _____
_____

5. _____
_____

6. _____
_____

7. _____
_____

8. _____

Reflection:

What did you learn from this activity?
_____
_____

How will what you learned make you a better listener?
_____
_____

Name _____ Date _____

Listening for the Truth

On the lines below, write one true statement and two untrue statements about yourself.

True: _____

_____

_____

Untrue: _____

_____

_____

Untrue: _____

_____

_____

Listen carefully as classmates take turns telling (NOT reading) their three statements to the class. Try to figure out which is the true statement.

How did you do? Were you able to correctly judge the statements?

_____

_____

Reflection:

What did you learn from this activity?

_____

_____

_____

How will what you learned make you a better listener?

_____

_____

_____

Name _____ Date _____

Comparing Notes of Two People Listening to the Same Thing

Try the following listening experiment. Your teacher will read a short story to you. Listen carefully.

Now that you have heard the story, write a brief summary of it below.

Summary of story:

_____
_____
_____
_____
_____
_____
_____
_____
_____

Now get with a partner. Compare your summary with that of your partner. Describe any similarities and any differences.

_____
_____
_____
_____

Reflection:

What did you learn from this activity?

_____
_____
_____

How will what you learned make you a better listener?

_____
_____

Listening Skills   Interviewing a Classmate

Name _____ Date _____

Interviewing a Classmate

Practice your listening skills by conducting an interview with one of your classmates. The interview topic will be "my favorite things." Ask your classmate each of the questions below and take some notes. When you have finished the interview, write a paragraph describing your classmate. Then have the classmate read the summary and give you feedback as to its accuracy.

Interview Questions:

1. What is your favorite television show and why? _____
_____
_____

2. What is your favorite book and why? _____
_____
_____

3. What is your favorite subject in school and why? _____
_____
_____

4. What is your favorite sport and why? _____
_____
_____

5. What is your favorite thing to do right after school and why? _____
_____
_____

6. What is your favorite thing to do on Saturdays and why? _____
_____
_____

7. What is your favorite animal and why? _____
_____
_____

8. What is your favorite movie and why? _____
_____
_____

© Mark Twain Media, Inc., Publishers

Listening Skills   Interviewing a Classmate

Name _____ Date _____

Summary paragraph of my classmate:

_____
_____
_____
_____
_____
_____
_____
_____
_____
_____
_____

Does your classmate think your summary is an accurate description of him or her? Why or why not?

_____
_____
_____

Reflection:

What did you learn from this activity?

_____
_____

How will what you learned make you a better listener?

_____
_____
_____

Listening Skills   Listening to Commercials

Name _____ Date _____

Listening to Commercials

The purpose of this activity is to gain practice in "listening with a purpose." Listening <u>for</u> something makes listening easier. You will listen to 10 different food commercials on television. As you listen to each commercial, record whether it mentions the following characteristics of the food being discussed: (1) how it tastes, (2) how much it costs, (3) what it looks like, (4) what it smells like, (5) how it feels, and (6) what it sounds like.

For each commercial, indicate the product and note the particular features mentioned.

1. Product: _____

Features mentioned: _____
_____

2. Product: _____

Features mentioned: _____
_____

3. Product: _____

Features mentioned: _____
_____

4. Product: _____

Features mentioned: _____
_____

5. Product: _____

Features mentioned: _____
_____

6. Product: _____

Features mentioned: _____
_____

7. Product: _____

Features mentioned: _____
_____

Listening Skills   Listening to Commercials

Name _____ Date _____

8. Product: _____

Features mentioned: _____

_____

9. Product: _____

Features mentioned: _____

_____

10. Product: _____

Features mentioned: _____

_____

Reflection:

What was difficult about this activity? _____

_____

_____

What was easy about this activity? _____

_____

_____

What did you learn from this activity? _____

_____

_____

How will what you learned make you a better listener? _____

_____

_____

_____

Listening Skills   Following Directions

Name _____   Date _____

Following Directions

In this activity, you will give 10 directions to a partner. These directions can be silly, simple, or whatever you decide, as long as the directions can be carried out in the classroom safely. For example, you might direct your partner to "go to the window and turn around twice." First, write down the 10 directions you want to give. Then read all 10 directions to your partner while he or she listens carefully and tries to remember them all and in the correct order.

Next, have your partner try to carry out each direction and in the proper order. As your partner does this, you should record in the right-hand column when he or she carries out the direction. Suppose direction #3 is "stand up." If that is the first direction carried out by your partner, write down "1" in the right-hand column on line 3 (for "stand up").

Directions: **Order Completed:**

1. _____   _____
2. _____   _____
3. _____   _____
4. _____   _____
5. _____   _____
6. _____   _____
7. _____   _____
8. _____   _____
9. _____   _____
10. _____   _____

Now evaluate how your partner did. How many of the 10 directions were carried out?
_____

How many of the directions were carried out at the appropriate point in the sequence?
_____

How could your partner have done a better job? _____
_____

Reflection:
What did you learn from this activity? _____
_____
_____

How will what you learned make you a better listener? _____
_____
_____
_____

Name _____   Date _____

Listening for Sounds All Around

While sitting in your classroom, listen carefully for five minutes and write down all the different types of sounds you hear (e.g., person's voice, car engine).

1. _____	11. _____	21. _____
2. _____	12. _____	22. _____
3. _____	13. _____	23. _____
4. _____	14. _____	24. _____
5. _____	15. _____	25. _____
6. _____	16. _____	26. _____
7. _____	17. _____	27. _____
8. _____	18. _____	28. _____
9. _____	19. _____	29. _____
10. _____	20. _____	30. _____

Count how many of the sounds fit into each of the following categories:

    Sounds outside your school building: _____

    Sounds inside the school building but outside your classroom: _____

    Sounds inside your classroom: _____

Now compare your list of sounds with the lists of your classmates.

Compared to your classmates, did you hear fewer or more sounds? _____

Why might that be so? _____

_____

_____

Did you record any sounds that your classmates did not? Why might that have happened?

_____

_____

Reflection:

What did you learn from this activity?

_____

_____

_____

How will what you learned make you a better listener?

_____

_____

_____

Listening Skills   Group Discussion

Name _____   Date _____

Group Discussion

In this activity, the class will have a discussion on the topic of "my favorite movies." Listen carefully as the discussion proceeds. When the teacher concludes the discussion, answer the questions below.

Group discussion reminders:
- **focus your attention on the main points**
- **take turns speaking**
- **include everyone**
- **listen to others' contributions**
- **disagree courteously**

1. What movies were named most frequently? _____
_____

2. Did all students like the same movies? Explain. _____
_____

3. Why did people like the movies they named? _____
_____

4. Did any students name scary movies as their favorite movies? If so, what movies were named? _____
_____

5. Did students discuss the topic courteously? (Circle Yes or No to the questions below.)
  - Did students take turns talking?   Yes   No
  - Did students stick to the point of the discussion?   Yes   No
  - Were all students encouraged to take part in the discussion?   Yes   No
  - Did students listen to each other?   Yes   No
  - Did students acknowledge that other students made good points?   Yes   No
  - Did students disagree without being disagreeable?   Yes   No

6. What things made listening difficult? _____
_____

Reflection:

What did you learn from this activity? _____
_____

How will what you learned make you a better listener? _____
_____

© Mark Twain Media, Inc., Publishers

Interviewing a "Listener" From Your Community

Name _____ Date _____

Your teacher has invited a member of your community to visit your class. After hearing the person speak about his or her job and after you have had a chance to ask the person some questions, fill in the blanks below.

Name of interviewee: _____

Interviewee's occupation: _____

Interviewee's place of employment: _____

Percentage of time interviewee spends listening in his or her work: _____

Why listening is important in the interviewee's line of work: _____

_____

_____

_____

_____

How the interviewee learned to be a good listener: _____

_____

_____

What could happen if the interviewee were not a good listener: _____

_____

_____

Reflection:

What did you learn from this activity? _____

_____

_____

How will what you learned make you a better listener? _____

_____

_____

_____

Listening Skills — Listening to the Evening News

Name _____ Date _____

Listening to the Evening News

Practice listening for information by listening to a television network's national evening news program.

Network listened to: _____ Date of broadcast: _____ Time: _____
Name of news anchor: _____
Names of other news reporters: _____
_____
Number of different news stories covered in the broadcast: _____
Number of stories about: crime _____   the economy _____   space _____
           sports _____   politics _____   religion _____   education _____
           health _____   race relations _____   disasters _____   other _____
Brief summary of lead (first) story: _____
_____
_____

U.S. cities mentioned and why: _____
_____

U.S. politicians mentioned and why: _____
_____

U.S. celebrities mentioned and why: _____
_____

Foreign countries mentioned and why: _____
_____

Most significant story (in your opinion) and why: _____
_____

Reflection:
What did you learn from this activity? _____
_____
_____

How will what you learned make you a better listener? _____
_____
_____

Listening Skills   Who Am I?

Name _____ Date _____

Who Am I?

1. On the "Mystery Student Clues" form, write five clues about yourself. Begin with clues that could describe other students as well as yourself and end with clues that more specifically describe you. Write your name on the "mystery student name" line.

2. Listen carefully as students take turns reading someone else's "Mystery Student Clues" to the class. Try to identify the mystery student being described. After the clues are read, write your prediction of the student's identity, and then write the actual identity after it is revealed.

Mystery Student Identities

	Prediction	Actual Identity		Prediction	Actual Identity
1.	_____	_____	13.	_____	_____
2.	_____	_____	14.	_____	_____
3.	_____	_____	15.	_____	_____
4.	_____	_____	16.	_____	_____
5.	_____	_____	17.	_____	_____
6.	_____	_____	18.	_____	_____
7.	_____	_____	19.	_____	_____
8.	_____	_____	20.	_____	_____
9.	_____	_____	21.	_____	_____
10.	_____	_____	22.	_____	_____
11.	_____	_____	23.	_____	_____
12.	_____	_____	24.	_____	_____

Reflection:

What did you learn from this activity?
_____
_____
_____

How will what you learned make you a better listener?
_____
_____
_____
_____

Listening Skills   Who Am I?

Name _____ Date _____

Mystery Student Clues

1. _____
2. _____
3. _____
4. _____
5. _____

Mystery Student's Name _____

---cutting line---

Mystery Student Clues

1. _____
2. _____
3. _____
4. _____
5. _____

Mystery Student's Name _____

---cutting line---

Mystery Student Clues

1. _____
2. _____
3. _____
4. _____
5. _____

Mystery Student's Name _____

Listening Skills   It's in the Bag!

Name _____ Date _____

It's in the Bag!

1. Bring to class a "mystery" object in a bag. The object should be something familiar to the other students and should be safe to bring to school. No live animals or valuable items should be used.

2. Think of three hints to describe your mystery object. These hints must be truthful but should not "give away" the answer. For example: Hint 1: It has a head. Hint 2: It has a tail. Hint 3: It fits in your pocket. Answer: A penny.

3. After listening to the hints, classmates should try to guess the identity of the mystery object.

Mystery Object in the Bag

Hint 1: _____
_____

Hint 2: _____
_____

HInt 3: _____
_____

    Mystery Object: _____

Reflection:

What did you learn from this activity?
_____
_____
_____

How will what you learned make you a better listener?
_____
_____
_____
_____

© Mark Twain Media, Inc., Publishers

Listening Skills   Listen to the Middle Man

Name _____ Date _____

Listen to the Middle Man

1. Find a partner. One of you will be the listener and the other will be the describer. The describer should sit facing the teacher. The listener should sit facing the describer, so that the teacher cannot be seen.

2. The teacher will hold up a common object. The describer will describe the object to the listener. Tell only what the object looks like; do not tell the purpose or name of the object. When the teacher puts the object down, the describer must stop talking.

3. The listener will now turn around and try to pick the object just described from several held up by the teacher.

4. Partners should change jobs and repeat the activity.

Were you able to identify the object from your partner's description? Why or why not?

_____
_____
_____

Was your partner able to identify the object from your description? Why or why not?

_____
_____
_____

Reflection:

What did you learn from this activity?

_____
_____
_____

How will what you learned make you a better listener?

_____
_____
_____

© Mark Twain Media, Inc., Publishers

Listening Skills • Poster-Making

Name _____ Date _____

Poster-Making

1. Working in groups of three, you will construct a copy of a poster made by the teacher.

2. One person in your group, the <u>Observer</u>, will look at the teacher-made poster, which will be kept outside the classroom (the poster station). The Observer is the only group member who may look at the teacher-made poster. The Observer will describe the poster to the second group member. The Observer must stay at the poster station.

3. The second group member, the <u>Listener</u>, is the only group member allowed to talk to the Observer. The Listener will describe the poster to the third group member. The Listener is the only group member who may walk to the poster station, the poster-making station (the poster-maker's desk in the classroom), and the supply table (in the classroom).

4. The third group member, the <u>Poster-Maker</u>, is the only group member allowed to talk to the Listener. The Poster-Maker will make a poster like the teacher's poster after hearing it described by the Listener. The Poster-Maker must stay at the poster-making station.

5. When your poster is finished, turn it face down and wait for the other groups to finish.

6. Compare each group's poster with the original.

How was your poster similar to the original poster? _____
_____
_____

How was your poster different from the original poster? _____
_____
_____

Why was your poster not exactly like the original poster? _____
_____
_____

Reflection:

What did you learn from this activity?
_____
_____
_____

How will what you learned make you a better listener?
_____
_____
_____

Listening Skills · When Nobody Listens

Name _____ Date _____

When Nobody Listens

1. Describe a time when you were speaking to someone, but that person was not listening carefully to you.

_____
_____
_____
_____

2. How did you know the person was not listening very well?

_____
_____
_____
_____

3. How did it make you feel when the other person did not listen to you?

_____
_____
_____
_____
_____

With a partner, carry out the following role-playing exercise. Each person should tell the other about "the most fun birthday you ever had," your "experiences at summer camp," or some other topic that you can easily talk about. Time your conversation so that you speak about the topic for three minutes. For half of that time, your partner should act disinterested and be a "poor listener." For the remaining half of the time, your partner should be an attentive, "good listener." Each of you should play the role of speaker and the role of listener.

Now that you have completed the exercise, describe the things you did when you were a good listener and when you were a poor listener. Then describe what your partner did.

Listening Skills   When Nobody Listens

Name _____ Date _____

4. When I was a good listener, I _____
_____
_____

5. When I was a poor listener, I _____
_____
_____

6. When my partner was a good listener, he or she _____
_____
_____

7. When my partner was a poor listener, he or she _____
_____
_____

Reflection:

What did you learn from this activity?

_____
_____
_____
_____

How will what you learned make you a better listener?

_____
_____
_____
_____

Name _____ Date _____

Listening or Not Listening?

Make a list of behaviors that indicate a student is paying attention to a speaker (for example, "The student is facing the speaker.").

1. _____
2. _____
3. _____
4. _____
5. _____
6. _____
7. _____

With the above list of behaviors in mind, one student should role play a situation in which he or she is listening or not listening. (Draw "Listening" or "Not Listening" from a basket.) Other students in the class should identify whether the student is listening or not listening by identifying the specific behaviors leading to such a conclusion.

Reflection:

What did you learn from this activity?

_____
_____
_____

How might what you learned make you a better listener?

_____
_____
_____

Listening Skills

Name That Word

Name _____ Date _____

Name That Word

1. Use a dictionary to help write short definitions of familiar words on the forms below. Cut the cards apart.

2. Everyone should listen while one student reads a definition. The student who is able to correctly name the word reads the next definition.

Definition:	Definition:
Word:	Word:

Definition:	Definition:
Word:	Word:

Definition:	Definition:
Word:	Word:

Definition:	Definition:
Word:	Word:

© Mark Twain Media, Inc., Publishers

Name _____ Date _____

Mixed-Up Charades

In this activity, students perform in pairs in front of the class.

1. One student begins by pretending to do something such as shoveling snow.

2. The second student asks, "What are you doing?".

3. The first student claims to be doing something else. For example, the student says, "I am brushing my teeth," while actually pretending to be shoveling snow.

4. The second student must begin pretending to do what the first student just said (brushing teeth).

5. The activity repeats as the first student now asks the second student, "What are you doing?".

6. The activity continues until one student does the wrong thing. Students should listen carefully and try to change activities smoothly and quickly.

Reflection:

What did you learn from this activity?

_____

_____

_____

How will what you learned make you a better listener?

_____

_____

_____

Trading Places Game

1. Students, sitting in a large circle of chairs, face the center of the room. One of the students acts as the announcer and stands inside the circle.

2. The announcer begins by giving a direction for a group of students to find a new seat. For example, he or she might say, "Anyone who has a younger brother, find another chair."

3. As students begin trading places, the announcer sits in an empty seat.

4. The student left without a chair becomes the announcer.

Reflection:

What did you learn from this activity?

_____

_____

_____

_____

How will what you learned make you a better listener?

_____

_____

_____

_____

Listening Skills   Who Said That Silly Sentence?

Name _____ Date _____

Who Said That Silly Sentence?

In this activity, one student sits at the front of the room with his or her back to the class. Another student, disguising his or her voice, reads a silly sentence. The first student tries to guess who read it. Listen carefully as the sentence is read. Can you recognize the voice? The guesser may have three tries to identify who read the sentence. If the guesser is successful, the reader becomes the next guesser. Here are some silly sentences students can read:

1. Your donkey is eating my lunch.
2. I looked up three stories down below me and saw King Arthur sitting at the fourth corner of a round table, eating vinegar with a fork.
3. She sells seashells down by the seashore.
4. If Peter Piper picked a peck of pickled peppers, how many peppers did Peter Piper pick?
5. How much wood could a woodchuck chuck if a woodchuck could chuck wood?
6. I can't believe I ate the whole thing twice.
7. Rubber baby buggy bumpers.
8. I shall now explain to Jane who hasn't got a brain how the rain in Spain falls mainly on the plain.
9. As the going gets tough, the tough get going, and as the rough needs mowing, the mowing gets rough.
10. I went out on a date, came home too late, came through a squeaky gate, threw up the meal I ate, and wished no one else my fate.

Reflection:

What did you learn from this activity?

_____

_____

_____

How might what you learned make you a better listener?

_____

_____

_____

© Mark Twain Media, Inc., Publishers

Listening Skills | Can You Answer Questions After Listening?

Name _____ Date _____

Can You Answer Questions After Listening?

In this activity, you can test your listening skills by listening to your teacher read a brief newspaper or magazine article. Listen carefully and then answer the questions below.

1. What would be a good title for the article?
   _____

2. What are the main ideas presented in the article?
   _____
   _____
   _____

3. Describe the purpose of the article.
   _____
   _____

4. Did you agree or disagree with what the article said? Explain.
   _____
   _____

5. What, if anything, in the article surprised you? Explain.
   _____
   _____

6. Was anything mentioned in the article that you did not understand? Explain.
   _____
   _____

7. What was the best thing about the article?
   _____
   _____

8. What was the worst thing about the article?
   _____
   _____

© Mark Twain Media, Inc., Publishers

Name _____ Date _____

9. Now that you have listened to the article, what questions do you have about the article or the topic discussed?

_____
_____
_____
_____
_____

Reflection:

What did you learn from this activity?

_____
_____

How will what you learned make you a better listener?

_____
_____
_____

Listening Skills | Famous Mystery Person

Name _____ Date _____

Famous Mystery Person

Research a famous person in order to find some interesting facts about that person's life. On the line below, write eight such facts about the person that you will read to your classmates. Your classmates will listen as you read each fact, and they will try to guess the identity of the famous mystery person using as few clues as possible. Make guessing more challenging by reading the least helpful clues first.

Clues:

1. _____
_____

2. _____
_____

3. _____
_____

4. _____
_____

5. _____
_____

6. _____
_____

7. _____
_____

8. _____
_____

Listen carefully as classmates take turns reading clues for their Famous Mystery Person. Write the name of each mystery person and the number of clues you needed to make a correct identification.

mystery person	# of clues needed	mystery person	# of clues needed
_____	_____	_____	_____
_____	_____	_____	_____
_____	_____	_____	_____

© Mark Twain Media, Inc., Publishers

Listening Skills   Famous Mystery Person

Name _____ Date _____

mystery person	# of clues needed	mystery person	# of clues needed
_____	_____	_____	_____
_____	_____	_____	_____
_____	_____	_____	_____
_____	_____	_____	_____
_____	_____	_____	_____
_____	_____	_____	_____
_____	_____	_____	_____
_____	_____	_____	_____
_____	_____	_____	_____
_____	_____	_____	_____
_____	_____	_____	_____
_____	_____	_____	_____
_____	_____	_____	_____
_____	_____	_____	_____

Reflection:

What did you learn from this activity?
_____
_____
_____

How will what you learned make you a better listener?
_____
_____
_____

Tips for the Teacher

- Be a good model. Show students that listening is important and show them how to do it.

- Praise good listening when it occurs. Discuss with students the advantages of good listening and the disadvantages of poor listening.

- Incorporate "listening carefully at all times" into a posted list of classroom rules. (Goldstein, 1988)

- To encourage good listening, give students a series of problems with oral directions. One such problem might be: "Start with the number 12, add 3, divide by 5, and subtract 1. What is the answer?" Do 20 such problems to encourage practice and assess improvement. Improvement might also be assessed over time by doing sets of similar problems once each week over several weeks. (Pratt, 1966)

- Have a "Let's Listen" week. During that week, have students do such things as: make posters (e.g., "Good Listening Habits"), incur "fines" for asking to have directions or instructions repeated, conduct experiments comparing the comprehension of something when reading it versus listening to it, work to eliminate distracting classroom noises, and present skits demonstrating some bad consequences of not listening. (Early, 1966)

- Encourage courtesy and attention in a fun, group, "story-telling" activity. One student begins by making up a short story. The next student continues the same story by giving two or three sentences that logically relate to the first student's story. This continues until every student has participated. (Early, 1966)

- Have students analyze commercials they have heard on television or the radio. Do students understand the purpose of the commercials? Can they distinguish between commercials that are based on emotional appeal only and those that offer "evidence" of a product's value? In the latter case, can students evaluate the credibility of that evidence?

- Whenever a guest speaks to the class, follow the presentation with (1) the instruction to write down the main points of the presentation, and (2) a class discussion of the presentation.

- To encourage students to listen for meaning, encourage them to raise their hands whenever they hear a word they do not understand. (Early, 1966)

- While listening is an activity for which students bear responsibility, there are things teachers can do to facilitate students' listening: (1) vary one's voice—the pitch, tone, and volume; (2) use gestures when speaking; (3) speak at a rate at which the most students possible can follow and comprehend; (4) strive to make presentations clear, understandable, interesting, and meaningful (for example, students tend to listen better when they see the personal relevance or usefulness of something); (5) inform students ahead of time that following a presentation, they will be questioned about it or asked to discuss it—this primes them to focus on listening; (6) stop occasionally and assess students' listening—can they repeat facts, summarize what has been said, and ask relevant questions?; (7) vary one's presentational style over the course of the day so that students are not overwhelmed by listening demands; students' attention can best be maintained when there is an occasional shift of activity (e.g., listening, to writing, to reading, to discussing, and so on); (8) point out to students when something is especially important, and the necessity of intensely concentrating; and (9) intersperse elements into a presentation that are sudden, unexpected, and unusual—a remark, a noise, and so on—things that tend to grab students' attention.

- It is as important for students to listen to each other as it is to listen to the teacher. Be sure to prompt, encourage, and reinforce both types of listening.

- Because background noise is an impediment to good listening, take steps to eliminate all classroom noise distractions. Realize that raising the volume of one's voice to overcome noise only adds to the overall noise level.

- Recognize that occasionally, a student's poor listening may be due to a physical problem that is causing a hearing deficit. If such a possibility is suspected, the student's hearing should be checked. If the problem cannot be corrected, it may be helpful for that student if the teacher uses a classroom audio amplification system. Other listening problems may be due to a student's attention deficit hyperactivity disorder. In such a case, teachers can seek consultation with the school counselor. A counselor may prove helpful, as well, for students who seem to not listen due to negative emotions associated with past listening experiences. Wolff and Marsnik (1992) suggest, for example, that a long-standing habit of not listening may arise as a result of a child "tuning out" parents who constantly nag and complain.

- Have students carry out the following activity: students working in pairs sit and face each other; student #1 speaks for five minutes on a topic of personal interest, while student #2 listens carefully, giving the speaker complete, undivided attention; after the five minutes, the listener, in his or her own words, reflects back to the speaker what was heard. At that point, the students switch roles. Stress to students the importance of making eye contact with the speaker, not interrupting, and so on. This can be a good activity for getting students to appreciate the value of gaining someone's undivided attention for a sustained period of time.

- Read a popular fable to the class. Tell students they should take notes while they listen because they will be asked to do two things with regard to the fable: (1) make an outline of the story, and (2) write a moral for the story.

- To help make listening a habit and something fun to do, incorporate games involving listening (like "Simon says" or "Mother, may I?") into "spare" moments in which doing anything else is difficult. The nice thing about such games is that the effectiveness of one's behavior hinges on careful listening and following the proper cues. Teachers might even take students beyond these games and discuss with them the general importance of "following orders" and the consequences of not doing so.

- Consider inviting to class professionals in the community who could talk to students about the importance of listening and the role that it plays in their work.

- Encourage good classroom listening with helpful prompts that cue students to pay attention. Verbal cues include statements like, "Pay close attention now, this is very important." Nonverbal cues include actions like turning off the classroom lights. Over time, students learn that such actions mean it is time to be quiet and listen.

- Try this activity to convince students that listening is not automatic, but rather requires active work on the listener's part. Say to students: "You are a race car driver driving a super-modified Ford Mustang. The track is hard, dry, and fast. The track record for the 200-mile race is one hour and 36 minutes. The wind is blowing with gusts up to 50 miles per hour. What is the race car driver's name?" Despite the fact that the answer to the question is given at the beginning of the statement, most students will not answer correctly. Use that fact to discuss how careful and attentive listeners have to be. (Hildebrandt, 1966)

- To test whether note-taking helps students or interferes with their listening, try the following experiment. Play 15 minutes of recorded lectures, speeches, or other material to the entire class. Half of the students should simply sit quietly and listen. The other half should sit quietly, listen, and take notes. Instruct those taking notes to write down the main ideas. After the presentation of the material, give students a test over the material. Compare the performance of the two groups and discuss the findings. (Barker, 1971)

- Encourage students to pick an acceptable day to remain silent all day—no talking and lots of listening. The exercise should make them more aware of how helpful and important listening can be. (Wolff & Marsnik, 1992)

- Try the following classroom experiment to demonstrate the importance of listening with a purpose (i.e., listening for answers to particular questions). Give a brief presentation to the class on any topic, but prior to the presentation, tell half the class to listen for specific types of information (e.g., the year something happened or the color of something). The other half of the class should be told only to listen carefully. Test students' recall of the critical information (i.e., the year, color, etc.) and compare the two groups to see if the prior instructions made a difference.

- Have students study oral advertisements, looking for examples of propaganda devices. Three such common devices are: (1) "always has, always will" fallacy: the false reasoning that just because something has existed or been done in the past, it is good and should justly be continued in the future; (2) the hasty generalization: reaching a conclusion on the basis of only a few cases; and (3) the hidden variable fallacy: the suggestion that just because two things follow in sequence, one therefore causes the other. (Barker, 1971; Wolff & Marsnik, 1992)

- Try the following "rumor game": Divide the class into two teams. Have the first person on each team silently read a sentence that has been written on a piece of paper. The first person then whispers the sentence to the next person on the team. The second person whispers it to the third person and so on until the last team member has heard the sentence. The last team member tells the sentence to the group. Compare the two teams to see who ended up with the most accurate version. Discuss with the class rumors and how rumors change in substance and why.

- In this activity, with a partner or with a small group, students will play, "I'm going on a trip and I will take….". Taking turns, each person adds an item to the growing list. Students should see how many items can be added to the list before someone cannot remember the entire list.

- Conduct the following experiment with the class: Split the class into three groups. Group 1 will read a selection of the teacher's choice (e.g., magazine article). Group 2 will listen to the teacher read the selection. Group 3 will read the selection themselves and will then listen to the teacher read the selection. Give all students the same recall test over details contained in the selection. Compare the performance of the three groups. The performance of Group 3 should be the best. Discuss with students the importance and advantage of not only reading a textbook assignment, but then reinforcing their knowledge by listening to the same or similar material being discussed in class by the teacher.

- The following experiment helps students see the importance of focusing attention on one thing (i.e., it is difficult to learn well when there are competing distractions). Make tape recordings of two different people giving a speech, making a presentation, giving the news, etc. Split the class into three groups. Group 1 will listen to only one of the recordings (Speaker 1). Group 2 will listen to both recordings simultaneously. Instruct Group 2 to listen carefully to both speakers. Group 3 will also listen to both recordings. Instruct Group 3 to listen carefully to Speaker 1. Give a recall test of the presentation of Speaker 1 to all students. Compare the performance of the groups. Group 1 should perform the best since they have no competing distractions. It should prove interesting to compare Group 2 and Group 3. While both had a competing distraction, Group 2 had the instruction to focus on both speakers. Did that instruction hurt their performance relative to Group 3? The results should make for a lively class discussion.

- The difficulty of concentrating on more than one thing at a time can also be demonstrated in very simple ways. For example, have students read a selection from one of their textbooks while they simultaneously write their names and addresses. From this and similar demonstrations, students should see that if they expect to remember what a speaker says, they must focus on the speaker's message and nothing else.

- Do the following activity in small groups. Each student makes a five-item list of (a) numbers, (b) foods, (c) popular songs, and (d) prominent personalities. Members of the groups take turns reading one of their lists (pausing about two seconds between items on the list). After reading a list, the student asks three questions about that list (e.g., "What was the second number listed?"). Every student keeps track of his or her own score by simply keeping a tally of correct versus incorrect answers. After all members of a group have read all of their lists, they can compare scores and declare a winner. (Wolff & Marsnik, 1992)

Answers to Listening Carefully Activity (page 27)
1) 11—add one post for the end
2) Same name as now, but the teacher was five years younger
3) the match
4) 51 are left
5) Neither—survivors were not buried
6) 12—all months have 28 days
7) halfway—then he is running out
8) yes—they do not celebrate our independence on that day, however

Sample Poster Ideas for Poster-Making Activity (page 44)
Possible materials for poster-making could include construction paper, newspapers, tag board, paper plates, markers, crayons, stickers, yarn, glue, or tape. The teacher-made model poster can be relatively simple, but be sure to have enough detail to make the activity interesting. All necessary supplies, including a few extra items, should be available for students at a supply table.

A sample poster might look similar to the one below.

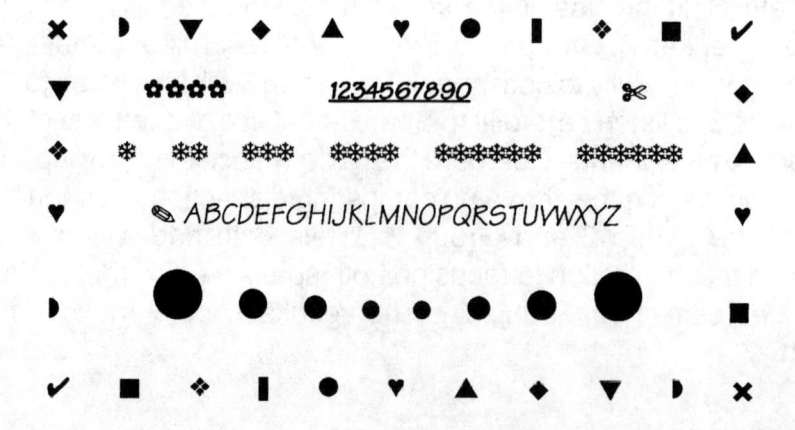

Bibliography

Barbara, D. A. (1958). *The art of listening* (2nd printing). Springfield, IL: Charles C. Thomas.

Barker, L. L. (1971). *Listening behavior.* Englewood Cliffs, NJ: Prentice-Hall.

Biehler, R. F., & Snowman, J. (1997). *Psychology applied to teaching* (8th ed.). Boston: Houghton Mifflin.

Charles, C. M. (1985). *Building classroom discipline: From models to practice* (2nd ed.). New York: Longman.

Dawis, R. V., & Fruehling, R. T. (1996). *Psychology: Realizing human potential* (8th ed.). St. Paul, MN: Paradigm.

Drakeford, J. (1967). *The awesome power of the listening ear.* Waco, TX: Word Books.

Duker, S. (Ed.) (1966). *Listening: Readings.* New York: The Scarecrow Press, Inc.

Early, M. J. (1966). Suggestions for teaching listening. In S. Duker (Ed.), *Listening: Readings* (pp. 211-18). New York: The Scarecrow Press, Inc.

Ellis, D. B. (1985). *Becoming a master student* (5th ed.). Rapid City, SD: College Survival, Inc.

Fenker, R. (1981). *Stop studying, start learning: Or how to jump-start your brain.* Fort Worth, TX: Tangram Press.

Goldstein, A. P. (1988). *The prepare curriculum: Teaching prosocial competencies.* Champaign, IL: Research Press.

Goleman, D. (1995). *Emotional intelligence.* New York: Bantam.

Goss, B. (1995). *The psychology of human communication* (2nd ed.). Prospect Heights, IL: Waveland Press, Inc.

Hildebrandt, H. W. (1966). Now hear this...some pointers on the neglected art of listening. In S. Duker (Ed.), *Listening: Readings* (pp. 389-93). New York: The Scarecrow Press, Inc.

Lewis, T. R., & Nichols, R. G. (1965). *Speaking and listening: A guide to effective oral-aural communication.* Dubuque, IA: Wm. C. Brown.

Nichols, M. P. (1995). *The lost art of listening*. New York: Guilford.

Osborn, M., & Osborn, S. (1994). *Public speaking* (3rd ed.). Boston: Houghton Mifflin.

Pratt, L. E. (1966). A lesson on following oral directions. In S. Duker (Ed.), *Listening: Readings* (pp. 230-33). New York: The Scarecrow Press, Inc.

Provonost, W., & Kingman, L. (1959). *The teaching of speaking and listening in the elementary school*. New York: David McKay Company, Inc.

Rogers, C. R. (1980). *A way of being*. Boston: Houghton Mifflin.

Russell, D. H., & Russell, E. F. (1959). *Listening aids through the grades: One hundred ninety listening activities*. New York: Columbia University.

Sylwester, R., & Cho, J. (1993). What brain research says about paying attention. *Educational leadership, 50*, 71-75.

Wang, M. C., Haertel, G. D., & Walberg, H. J. (1994). What helps students learn? *Educational Leadership, 51*, 74-79.

Williams, R., & Williams, V. (1993). *Anger kills: Seventeen strategies for controlling the hostility that can harm your health*. New York: Times Books.

Williams, R. L., & Long, J. D. (1983). *Toward a self-managed lifestyle* (3rd ed.). Boston: Houghton Mifflin.

Wolff, F. I., & Marsnik, N. C. (1992). *Perceptive listening* (2nd ed.). Fort Worth, TX: Harcourt Brace Jovanovich.